CQ/inVerse

MW01615631

Nehemiah: Principles of
Biblical Leadership

October–December 2019

Staff
Editor: Justin Kim
Senior Editorial Assistant: Sikhu Daco
Director of Sabbath School: Ramon Canals
Assoc. Director of Sabbath School: Jim Howard
Design and Illustration: Types & Symbols

Principal Contributor: Editorial Staff

Editorial Office: Sabbath School & Personal Ministries
Department, General Conference of Seventh-day
Adventists, 12501 Old Columbia Pike, Silver Spring,
MD 20904-6600, USA.

Place orders with Pacific Press® Publishing Association,
P.O. Box 5353, Nampa, ID 83653-5353, USA.

Other than the King James Version, Scripture versions
used in this Bible study guide are as follows:

CQ/inVerse is published quarterly by the General
Conference of Seventh-day Adventists, 12501 Old
Columbia Pike, Silver Spring, MD, 20904, USA, and
printed by Pacific Press® Publishing Association, 1350
North Kings Road, Nampa, ID 83687-3193, USA.

One-year subscription in USA, $39.96; single copy,
$9.99. One-year subscription in countries outside
USA, $47.96. All prices at USA exchange.

Printed in the USA.
ISBN 978-0-8163-6599-9

Contents

Nehemiah: Principles of Biblical Leadership

About Inverse

Philosophy

The inVerse Bible Study Guide curriculum has been developed for those who yearn for a more profound Bible study experience. It will dare you to engage Scripture more deeply and more broadly, ultimately enriching the ability to share your growing experience with others. Everything from the content to the format has been designed to enhance your spiritual journey if you will accept the challenge of engaging this Bible study.

Format

There will be two formats: the Journal edition that utilizes digital space and the Print edition that is abridged for traditional users. If you page through the Journal edition, you will immediately be struck by how much blank space there is! No, we did not forget to print the text, nor are we simply trying to save money on ink. The space has been intentionally left open for you to fill-in with your personal study of the Bible. The margins provide guidance on how to engage the text for study and you will document your experience with Scripture in the journaling space provided.

Numerous studies have shown that writing out by hand your thoughts, reflections, and engagement with the text will deepen their kinesthetic impression on your mind. Something about putting pen to paper helps tactilely internalize the material. No, it's not the same as typing it out! We certainly benefit from the unlimited space of the digital world, but we should not be slaves to its limitations. So take the time to write in those open spaces. Don't worry if your handwriting is terrible! This Journal is for your own record, so just make sure it's legible to you.

On that note, this Journal will be a resource for you to reference anytime you need to share a Bible study, preach a sermon, or refresh yourself on the particular Bible topic. Place inVerse on your bookshelf; as you continue through the curriculum, enjoy the aesthetic appeal of the curriculum on display in your personal library.

Content

Four inVerse Bible Study Guides will be produced each year. Twice a year, the topics covered will correlate with the topics presented in the Adult Bible Study Guide (ABSG). Even then, while the topic for the quarter may be similar to that of the ABSG, the specific weekly material will differ. The remaining two topics for the year will not mirror the ABSG, but will be specially selected to address young adults.

While the inVerse curriculum is intended primarily for the young adult Sabbath School experience, it can also be used as a versatile tool for personal ministry application. There are no dates printed, so that you can use and reuse this resource anytime with anyone. There are also no days of the week; so if, for instance, you have a small group Bible discussion on a Wednesday evening, you could make Thursday your first day of study that culminates in a group discussion the following Wednesday. The discussion questions at the end of the weekly lesson (entitled inQuire) will help stimulate your small group discussion whenever you hold it.

A notable change is the sparse commentary included. Removing the commentary in the Journal edition is intended to encourage personal Bible study, rather than relying on someone else's comments from their Bible study. There is commentary available online, accessible through the QR codes in your study guide. However, just as the discussion with your small group only enhances your Bible study, the online commentary is mean to augment your understanding throughout the week.

Benefits

In summary, some benefits of the inVerse Bible Study Guide curriculum include:

- Deepening your identity as a Christ-centered, Bible-believing, and Advent-awaiting Christian
- Learning how to study the Bible for yourself
- Generating your own Bible studies for use in sharing
- Teaching others how to Bible study and Bible journal
- Understanding the Bible topics better since having developed the material yourself
- Participating in a more lively small group Bible discussion based on advance preparation
- Stretching your faculties by engaging both the analog and the digital in your study
- Hearing fewer opinions and more of what the Bible actually says on topics
- Knowing, loving, and serving the Lord Jesus Christ more fully

Finally, it may take a bit more effort on your part to feel the benefits of this new curriculum, but the effort will be well worth it. Pray earnestly for the aid of the Holy Spirit as you wrestle with some texts, or as you learn the discipline of consistently meditating on the Word of God. Allow God to teach you and to mold you as you engage Scripture and you will not regret it.

A Quick Guide to Usage

1. Pray seriously and honestly!
2. Read with a digital or analog Bible (it's a Bible study guide—don't skim over the Bible parts!)
3. Use your favorite writing utensil for the analog Journal components.
4. In the Journal edition, scan the QR code for more commentary and resources on the text.
5. Use inVerse either for daily devotions (seven steps for seven days; 13 weeks for every three months) or for weekly Bible study, Sabbath School, prayer meeting, family worships, or discipleship on how to study the Bible

Study Guide Sections

 inTro—introduces the passage of the week as well as its main themes

 inScribe—provides a prompt to write out the text

 inGest—focuses on practical points, reflective principles, and contextual details

 inTerpret—focuses on more apologetic perspectives and questions that might arise from the passage

 inSpect—provides a list of verses outside the main passage to be cross-studied for deeper insight and clarity

 inVite—centers the passage and its principles on bringing out and pointing to Jesus Christ, the living Word

 inSight—presents a perspective from the writings of Ellen White on the passage or theme

 inQuire—introduces a list of questions to be answered reflectively or used as a resource for discussion (in a Sabbath School class, for instance)

Further Study Resources

Users are also encouraged to watch inVerse on Hope Channel TV (https://www.hopetv.org/inverse) for the corresponding lesson. This online roundtable discussion seeks to study the Bible with warm humor, practical intelligence, simple application, and authenticity. May you be blessed as you embark on this experience and as the Holy Spirit opens your mind and heart to Him.

inVerse is a publication of the Sabbath School and Personal Ministries Department of the General Conference of Seventh-day Adventists for university students, young adults, working professionals, and young parents.

Introduction to Nehemiah: Principles of Biblical Leadership

Leadership in secular contexts denotes power, position, fame, and wealth. Leaders have been known to seduce, force, penalize, and calculate. These qualities contrast with the life and teachings of Jesus Christ, who taught meekness, humility, and spirituality. Although He never traveled extensively, won a military battle, or wrote a magnum opus, He was the greatest leader the world has ever seen. While the Bible portrays many wonderful leaders, they all point to Jesus, the composite picture of biblical leadership. One of these biblical characters embodied the character and spirituality of Christ while executing results efficiently, accomplishing the goals of a vision, and achieving success. Like a leadership manual, the story of Nehemiah reveals the principles of biblical leadership.

While global corporations, legal and government organizations, and military or sports campaigns have clear material objectives, the book of Nehemiah presents leadership from a different perspective altogether: the kingdom of God. Rather than the use of hard power, the leadership that is based on a noble character is presented and ultimately reflects the person of Jesus. This type of leadership asks a particular set of questions: How does God deal with sin? How does He reconcile His innate hatred for sin and His intense love for sinners? What is His plan to save the world? What is the role of the Christian in the midst of this world?

These questions become real in the life of a university student, in the professional setting, in positions of leadership, and in our roles as parents, where the principles of the kingdom of God are many times eclipsed by worldly pursuits. How are Christians supposed to live in this modern world? How are Christians to lead others while maintaining a humble, devotional life with the Lord? Does the Bible give practical insights into these questions?

Rather than using psychological tricks of seduction, playbooks of cunning strategy, and power tactics of intimidation, Christians are called to be proponents of change in the world simply through their characters and godly leadership. In other words, Christians lead others by being led by God. While secular methods of leadership may be motivated by profit, power, and ambition, the book of Nehemiah presents principles to experience the joy of doing God's will and making His glory known to the entire world.

Principles are absolutely necessary to guide Christians to lead other individuals, families, organizations, and even nations to do and live out the will of God. Finding these guiding principles requires prayer, time, study, and wisdom. Once they find these principles of biblical leadership, readers will be able to use them in any field of study or work.

As we study with this guide on biblical leadership, may we keep the glory of God in mind and endeavor to apply its practical principles in real time. This text will bless those who keep a humble heart, a diligent mind, and a seeking spirit. Through this book, we will learn how to plan our work, organize our time and resources, prioritize our duties, motivate those whom we are leading, and hopefully, obtain heavenly results. We will also glimpse the secret weapons of Christian leaders, the steps to handle opposition, and the heavenly courage needed for difficult situations. May we find the answers to our questions; follow the greatest leader, Jesus, even more closely; and be able to lead whatever, whomever, and whenever He calls.

Discovery of Calling:
Prayer and Purpose
Nehemiah 1

Week One

inTro

Read This Week's Passage:
Nehemiah 1

STAYING BEHIND

The Babylonian army had conquered Judah as well as the majority of the then-known world, bringing captives to its capital city. After the death of its king Nebuchadnezzar, Babylon fell to the rising Medo-Persian Empire. Their more lenient government allowed exiles to return to their homelands. The book of Ezra (which was once bound together with the book of Nehemiah) recalls this edict and describes the progression of the Judean reconstruction. At this time, we find Nehemiah did not return back to his homeland. Instead, he served in the royal courts of Susa.

The books of Ezra, Esther, Haggai, Zechariah, Malachi, and possibly others, also called post-exilic, take place after the Babylonian invasion of Judah and the Babylonian Exile. Be mindful that these books do not appear in chronological order. By the time of Nehemiah, reconstruction and rebuilding had already occurred in Jerusalem, but due to opposition and internal conflicts, the work was not finished.

In the opening of the account of the book, Nehemiah is found to be in the Medo-Persian winter citadel palace of Shushan, or Susa (the same place as the Ahasuerus's great feast in Esther 1 and the vision of Daniel 8). The year is the twentieth into the reign of King Artaxerxes and the month is Chisleu, around November-December. Though these background details seem unimportant, they are crucial in understanding the narrative and extracting principles of leadership for our individual spheres.

Write out Nehemiah 1 from the translation of your choice. If you're pressed for time, write out Nehemiah 1:4–11. You may also rewrite the passage in your own words, outline it, or mind map the chapter.

inGest

Go back to your scribed text and study the passage.

(Circle) repeated words/phrases/ideas

Underline words/phrases that are important and have meaning to you

Draw **Arrows** to connect words/phrases to other associated or related words/phrases

$\longrightarrow$

Memorize your favorite verse. Write it out multiple times to help memorization.

What is your prayer life like? What promises can you claim for situations in your life? Do you have a vision for your role in God's work?

Read more at
www.inversebible.org/neh1-3

inTerpret

After looking at your scribed and annotated text, what special insights do your marks overall seem to point to?

←————————————————

What questions emerge after studying this passage? What parts are difficult?

What other principles and conclusions do you find?

Read more at
www.inversebible.org/neh1-4

inSpect

How do the following verses relate to the primary passage?

Ezra 4:4–24
Leviticus 26:27–45
2 Chronicles 6:26–39

———————————→

What other verses/promises come to mind in connection with Nehemiah 1?

Review your memorized verse from Nehemiah 1.

inVite

Meditate on Nehemiah 1 again and look for Jesus in the passage.

←——————————

What parallels do you see between Nehemiah's intercession and Christ's intercession?

How do you see Jesus differently or see Him again?

Prayer: How do you respond to seeing Jesus in this way?

Read more at
www.inversebible.org/neh1-6

inSight

Review your memory verse. How does it apply to your life this week?

———————→

As you have studied this week, what personal applications have you been convicted of in your life?

What are practical applications you must make in your school, family, workplace, and church?

Read more inSight from the Spirit of Prophecy at www.inversebible.org/neh1-7

inQuire

Share insights from this week's memory verse and Bible study as well as any discoveries, observations, and questions with your Sabbath School class (or Bible study group). Consider these discussion questions with the rest of the group.

←——————————————→

What are some burdens that God is putting on your heart?

What walls are breaking down around you now and need to be repaired?

What are some human needs around you that you are being called to serve?

How can we place more care, concern, and investment into humanity as Nehemiah did for his people who were so far away?

What palatial luxuries are we encompassed with?

What is your life burden?

What is your life passion?

What is your life calling?

Do these three intersect? Why, or why not?

In His Presence: Vision and Planning

Nehemiah 2:1–9

inTro

Read This Week's Passage:
Nehemiah 2:1–9

BETWEEN FOUR AND FIVE

Sometimes we gloss over the seemingly unimportant details of Scripture. But once understood, these details can provide great insights. If we compare the first verse of Nehemiah 1 to the first verse of chapter 2, we see that chapter 2 also takes place in the twentieth year of King Artaxerxes' reign. The month Chisleu of chapter 1 is the equivalent of November-December of the Gregorian calendar, while the month of Nisan (not the Japanese automobile corporation) of chapter 2 was about March-April of the Gregorian calendar. So, these apparently superfluous details portray that Nehemiah prayed and fasted for four to five months. In order words, God answered his prayers not in decades or years but in a few months (although some of us cannot imagine waiting months for an answer to a prayer!).

Do you have any large decisions that you need to make—for instance, decisions concerning your career, calling, lifework, marriage, or finding your purpose in life? Why not set aside some time to pray and fast for the Lord's wisdom and intervention? It may be a shorter time than you anticipate, perhaps four to five months, before you notice Heaven moving circumstances in your life as a response.

inScribe

Write out Nehemiah 2:1–9 from the translation of your choice. If you're pressed for time, write out Nehemiah 2:2–6. You may also rewrite the passage in your own words, outline it, or mind map the chapter.

inGest

Go back to your scribed text and study the passage.

Circle repeated words/phrases/ideas

Underline words/phrases that are important and have meaning to you

Draw **Arrows** to connect words/phrases to other associated or related words/phrases

Memorize your favorite verse. Write it out multiple times to help memorization.

Where is tact needed in your life? How do you cultivate tactful communication without being manipulative? Are you tactful in your family interactions?

Read more at
www.inversebible.org/neh2-3

inTerpret

After looking at your scribed and annotated text, what special insights do your marks overall seem to point to?

←——————————————

What questions emerge after studying this passage? What parts are difficult?

What other principles and conclusions do you find?

Read more at
www.inversebible.org/neh2-4

inSpect

What relationship do the following verses have with the primary passage?

1 Thess. 5:17; Exod. 4:15
Matt. 10:16
Acts 26:24–31

———————————→

What other verses/promises come to mind in connection with Nehemiah 2:1–9?

Review your memorized verse from Nehemiah 2:1–9.

inVite

Meditate on Nehemiah 2:1–9 again and look for Jesus in the passage.

←———————————

Is Jesus tactful and strategic in the way He operates?

How do you see Jesus differently or see Him again?

Prayer: How do you respond to seeing Jesus in this way?

Read more at
www.inversebible.org/neh2-6

inSight

Review your memory verse.
How does it apply to your
life this week?

⟶

As you have studied this
week, what personal
applications have you been
convicted of in your life?

What are practical applications
you must make in your school,
family, workplace, and church?

Read more inSight from the
Spirit of Prophecy at
www.inversebible.org/neh2-7

inQuire

Share insights from this week's memory verse and Bible study as well as any discoveries, observations, and questions with your Sabbath School class (or Bible study group). Consider these discussion questions with the rest of the group.

←――――――――――――――――

What is the relationship between prayer and action?

What are the extremes of too much prayer and too much action?

Is tact necessary? How can you develop your tactfulness?

What is the difference between tact and deceit?

Are planning, logistics, and strategy spiritual gifts?

Why is planning not a demonstration of a lack of faith?

How are spirituality and occupation related to each other?

How has God used individuals in high positions of society in the past?

How can you access resources in the world and harness them for the proclamation of the gospel?

The Hand of God

Nehemiah 2:10–20

inTro

Read This Week's Passage:
Nehemiah 2:10–20

MOVING ON

When God moves in your life, it is one thing to enjoy the experience by yourself; it is another thing to share the experience with others around you. In the story of Nehemiah, God had worked out miracles in Nehemiah's secular context to advance his religious goals. Nehemiah had received all the things that were needed to rebuild the wall. From the small details to the large logistical concerns, materials and diplomatic clearance were not only boldly requested but also astonishingly granted.

But now, more important than the project itself, Nehemiah was called to rally God's people, the people of Jerusalem, to rebuild the city walls. After years of sluggish progress, it was not only the wall that needed to be rebuilt but the confidence of the public. The testimony of the heavenly King touching the heart of the earthly king was evidence that the hand of God was upon Nehemiah. He made sure that the people heard this story and used it to encourage their faith to rebuild once again. If earthly powers were moving, how much more the heavenly powers that were behind them?

Write out Nehemiah 2:10–20 from the translation of your choice. If you're pressed for time, write out Nehemiah 2:16–18. You may also rewrite the passage in your own words, outline it, or mind map the chapter.

inGest

Go back to your scribed text and study the passage.

(**Circle**) repeated words/ phrases/ideas

Underline words/phrases that are important and have meaning to you

Draw **Arrows** to connect words/ phrases to other associated or related words/phrases

⟶

Memorize your favorite verse. Write it out multiple times to help memorization.

Are you experiencing antagonism in your life? How do you respond to antagonism from your family? What factors help you to persevere when the odds are against you?

Read more at
www.inversebible.org/neh3-3

inTerpret

After looking at your scribed and annotated text, what special insights do your marks overall seem to point to?

←————————————

What questions emerge after studying this passage? What parts are difficult?

What other principles and conclusions do you find?

Read more at
www.inversebible.org/neh3-4

The Hand of God

inSpect

What relationship do the following verses have with Nehemiah 2:10–20?

Prov. 6:6–8
Prov. 16:9
Luke 14:28–33

———————————→

What other verses/promises come to mind in connection with Nehemiah 2:10–20?

Review your memorized verse from Nehemiah 2:10–20.

inVite

Meditate on Nehemiah 2:10–20 again and look for Jesus in the passage.

←——————————————

Could Nehemiah have accomplished his goals without Christ's aid?

How do you see Jesus differently or see Him again?

Prayer: How do you respond to seeing Jesus in this way?

Read more at
www.inversebible.org/neh3-6

The Hand of God

inSight

Review your memory verse. How does it apply to your life this week?

⟶

As you have studied this week, what personal applications have you been convicted of in your life?

What are practical applications you must make in your school, family, workplace, and church?

Read more inSight from the Spirit of Prophecy at www.inversebible.org/neh3-7

inQuire

Share insights from this week's memory verse and Bible study as well as any discoveries, observations, and questions with your Sabbath School class (or Bible study group). Consider these discussion questions with the rest of the group.

←————————————————

What experiences has God given you that you have already shared with others to encourage them?

What experiences has God given you that you have not shared with others? Why have you not shared?

What is the danger of only believing another's report of a situation?

What principles of witnessing and tact can we learn from Nehemiah's experience?

What are the principles of biblical leadership for eliciting people's support?

What are the principles of leadership in handling opposition?

What walls in your life need rebuilding?

How does one balance the emphasis between the people and the project?

The Hand of God

Organized to Orchestrate

Nehemiah 3

inTro

Read This Week's Passage:
Nehemiah 3

BRICK AFTER BRICK

Warning: this chapter can be categorized as one of the lackluster chapters in the Bible. Just like building a wall, brick after brick, chapter 3 of Nehemiah details the people involved, verse after verse. Even so, many principles of biblical leadership can be gleaned from this seemingly monotonous passage. Even before you scribe the passage, there are some preliminary lessons to be learned:

1. Persevere through the "boring" parts of the Bible. It may be that we are not ready for some particular grain of truth at some specific stage of our spiritual experience. But precious gems of truth await if we will patiently wade through and endure the reading

2. Readers do not always have to get something out of the Bible. Sometimes these details are background information or a setup for another story. As with all relationships, one does not have to get something out of everything.

3. In the "me-centeredness" of our culture, we fail to realize that it's not always about God squeezing into our narrative, but about us squeezing into His plan to save the world. Some parts of the Bible have seemingly obscure names and details, but they are recorded in the Bible, the inspired Word of God!

4. Though there is nothing special about each brick, an amazing structure emerges when one is done laying them down to build a wall. May we read this chapter with Nehemiah's patience and diligence.

Write out Nehemiah 3 from the translation of your choice. If you're pressed for time, write out Nehemiah 3:1–5. You may also re write the passage in your own words, outline it, or mind map the chapter. Follow the graphic to visualize the city walls.

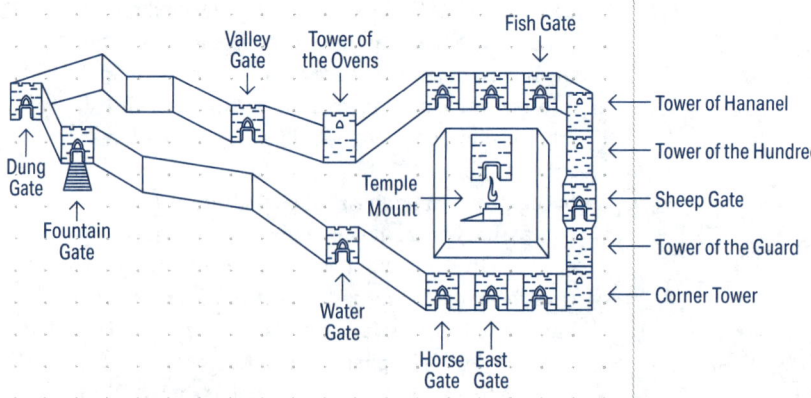

inGest

Go back to your scribed text and study the passage.

 repeated words/phrases/ideas

__Underline__ words/phrases that are important and have meaning to you

Draw **Arrows** to connect words/phrases to other associated or related words/phrases

Memorize your favorite verse. Write it out multiple times to help memorization.

What type of builder are you? How does your work ethic impact others?

Read more at
www.inversebible.org/neh4-3

inTerpret

After looking at your scribed and annotated text, what special insights do your marks overall seem to point to?

←——————————————

What questions emerge after studying this passage? What parts are difficult?

What other principles and conclusions do you find?

Read more at
www.inversebible.org/neh4-4

Organized to Orchestrate

inSpect

What relationship do the following verses have with the primary passage?

Prov. 22:29
1 Cor. 12:12–26
Gal. 3:28

——————————→

What other verses/promises come to mind in connection with Nehemiah 3?

Review your memorized verse from Nehemiah 3.

Meditate on Nehemiah 3 again and look for Jesus in the passage.

←——————————

Based on John 5:39, what does the fact that Nehemiah 3 is part of Scripture reveal about Jesus?

How do you see Jesus differently or see Him again?

Prayer: How do you respond to seeing Jesus in this way?

Read more at
www.inversebible.org/neh4-6

Organized to Orchestrate

inSight

Review your memory verse. How does it apply to your life this week?

→

As you have studied this week, what personal applications have you been convicted of in your life?

What are practical applications you must make in your school, family, workplace, and church?

Read more inSight from the Spirit of Prophecy at www.inversebible.org/neh4-7

inQuire

Share insights from this week's memory verse and Bible study as well as any discoveries, observations, and questions with your Sabbath School class (or Bible study group). Consider these discussion questions with the rest of the group.

←——————————————

What are some tips to help read through the more difficult parts of Scripture?

Are you a Tekoite or a Tekoite noble?

Why do people seek recognition? Is it wrong to seek recognition? Is there a biblical way to do it?

How can our secular work interface with our spiritual work?

Is being organized a character trait or a learned skill? Why?

How can you tap into Nehemiah's enthusiasm?

Why and how does God use organizations?

Are being organized and being controlling the same thing?

Is being disorganized a vice? Why?

How do you fit into the larger picture of what God is trying to do?

Organized to Orchestrate

Through External Opposition: Prayer

Nehemiah 4:1–6

inTro

Read This Week's Passage:
Nehemiah 4:1–6

NEWTON'S THIRD LAW

Every action has an equal and opposite reaction in the realm of physics. But the same occurs in the spiritual realm. When there is movement going forward, there is also friction moving against it. In leadership, any project is bound to undergo opposition before it meets success.

While God's people are rallying behind Nehemiah in chapter 2 and uniting to build the wall in chapter 3, chapter 4 gives us insight into what their enemies were doing. God was not the only One moving—His enemy was too. A coalition had been forming against Nehemiah's initiative. Sanballat, the governor of Samaria (northern region); Tobiah the Ammonite (an eastern region); Geshem the Arabian king (a southern region); and the Ashdodites (west of Israel) created an alliance to surround Jerusalem. Trace the growth of their coalition from Nehemiah 2:10, 19, and 4:7. They could not war openly against Jerusalem because Nehemiah was under the protection of the king. Rather, in Nehemiah 4, they implemented three strategies: ridicule (4:1–3), violence (4:7, 8), and discouragement (4:11, 12).

In this week's study, we find the biblical answer to external forms of opposition: prayer. It sounds like a simple answer, but it really is the ultimate means to overcome any challenge. Instead of letting emotion take over, Nehemiah resorted to prayer. He did not repress his frustrations or express them to others. Instead, he confessed his heart to the Lord and then reassessed his situation. This focus allowed the people to have confidence in their leader and to mimic his restraint and resolve.

inScribe

Write out Nehemiah 4:1–6 from the translation of your choice. If you're pressed for time, write out Nehemiah 4:4–6. You may also rewrite the passage in your own words, outline it, or mind map the chapter.

inGest

Go back to your scribed text and study the passage.

 repeated words/ phrases/ideas

Underline words/phrases that are important and have meaning to you

Draw **Arrows** to connect words/ phrases to other associated or related words/phrases

Memorize your favorite verse. Write it out multiple times to help memorization.

What insecurities do you struggle with? How do your insecurities impact your family? How can Christ help you overcome your insecurities?

Read more at
www.inversebible.org/neh5-3

inTerpret

After looking at your scribed and annotated text, what special insights do your marks overall seem to point to?

←——————————————

What questions emerge after studying this passage? What parts are difficult?

What other principles and conclusions do you find?

Read more at
www.inversebible.org/neh5-4

inSpect

What relationship do the following verses have with the primary passage?

Prov. 16:32
Rom. 8:31
2 Cor. 12:9

→

What other verses/promises come to mind in connection with Nehemiah 4:1–6?

Review your memorized verse from Nehemiah 4:1–6.

Meditate on Nehemiah 4:1–6 again and look for Jesus in the passage.

←——————————

Are you comfortable with the concept of Jesus punishing the wicked?

How do you see Jesus differently or see Him again?

Prayer: How do you respond to seeing Jesus in this way?

Read more at
www.inversebible.org/neh5-6

Through External Opposition: Prayer

inSight

Review your memory verse. How does it apply to your life this week?

→

As you have studied this week, what personal applications have you been convicted of in your life?

What are practical applications you must make in your school, family, workplace, and church?

Read more inSight from the Spirit of Prophecy at www.inversebible.org/neh5-7

inQuire

Share insights from this week's memory verse and Bible study as well as any discoveries, observations, and questions with your Sabbath School class (or Bible study group). Consider these discussion questions with the rest of the group.

←——————————————

Have you ever been personally attacked?

How have you dealt with similar social and/or spiritual situations in the past? Which party were you?

Can things go wrong for people who live right? If so, what can we say to give them comfort and courage?

What are the tools of the devil mentioned in this chapter?

How has prayer solved your situations of opposition?

Are our spiritual lives so close with God that we identify with Him in everything, even to the extent that we imprecate others?

How is God like a Lamb and a Lion?

How do we explain the imprecatory prayers in the Bible?

Through External Opposition: Watchfulness

Nehemiah 4:7–23

inTro

Read This Week's Passage:
Nehemiah 4:7–23

COURAGE BY CONFLICT

Nehemiah 4–6 can be taken as a narrative that compiles the schemes of the opposition. The first chapter of this section recounts forms of direct external opposition. Chapter 5 reframes opposition from an internal perspective, where issues arise from the people within. The last chapter revisits external opposition but now from an indirect, hidden angle. Three whole chapters dedicated to opposition, indicating that friction and resistance should not discourage godly leaders. Whenever God moves, there will always be a reaction from the devil. We should, in fact, be encouraged when there is friction. For when there is friction, we can rest assured that there is movement.

These opposition chapters advise us on the recourse we can take when faced with opposition. There is nothing new under the sun, and today's attacks still fall into these categories. As the study of these chapters will reveal, the opposition is not the challenge. The real challenge is to consistently, persistently, insistently, and faithfully turn to God at each point of conflict. Last week's study identified the main weapon for biblical leadership as prayer. This week, we will look at the second weapon against external opposition.

Write out Nehemiah 4:7–23 from the translation of your choice. If you're pressed for time, write out Nehemiah 4:9, 13–17. You may also rewrite the passage in your own words, outline it, or mind map the chapter.

inGest

Go back to your scribed text and study the passage.

 repeated words/ phrases/ideas

Underline words/phrases that are important and have meaning to you

Draw **Arrows** to connect words/ phrases to other associated or related words/phrases

⟶

Memorize your favorite verse. Write it out multiple times to help memorization.

How do you deal with discouragement? How can you help others overcome discouragement in their lives?

Read more at
www.inversebible.org/neh6-3

inTerpret

After looking at your scribed and annotated text, what special insights do your marks overall seem to point to?

←

What questions emerge after studying this passage? What parts are difficult?

What other principles and conclusions do you find?

Read more at
www.inversebible.org/neh6-4

inSpect

What relationship do the following verses have with the primary passage?

Luke 21:34–36
Eph. 6:18
Phil. 2:13

⟶

What other verses/promises come to mind in connection with Nehemiah 4:7–23?

Review your memorized verse from Nehemiah 4:7–23.

inVite

Meditate on Nehemiah 4:7–23 again and look for Jesus in the passage.

←——————————————

How does Jesus fight for us when we are the ones who have the swords in hand?

How do you see Jesus differently or see Him again?

Prayer: How do you respond to seeing Jesus in this way?

Read more at
www.inversebible.org/neh6-6

Through External Opposition: Watchfulness

inSight

Review your memory verse. How does it apply to your life this week?

———————→

As you have studied this week, what personal applications have you been convicted of in your life?

What are practical applications you must make in your school, family, workplace, and church?

Read more inSight from the Spirit of Prophecy at www.inversebible.org/neh6-7

inQuire

Share insights from this week's memory verse and Bible study as well as any discoveries, observations, and questions with your Sabbath School class (or Bible study group). Consider these discussion questions with the rest of the group.

←——————————

Describe the last time you were really discouraged. By whom, when, where, how, and why were you discouraged?

How did you get out of discouragement?

What is the individual's responsibility when it comes to the morale of the larger group?

Who is absolved of this responsibility?

What things can leaders do to raise the morale of the church?

Is being distracted a social or a spiritual problem?

How can the level of sacrifice be raised today by the leadership?

How can we watch and pray?

Where does the principle of divine cooperation need to be exercised in your life?

Through External Opposition: Watchfulness

The Usage of Power
Nehemiah 5

inTro

Read This Week's Passage:
Nehemiah 5

TEMPTATIONS OF LEADERSHIP

Whether it's by appointment, accomplishment, election, perception, or ability, when individuals are called to serve, they are called to leadership regardless of title. They may not be up front, calling the shots and directing the masses—traffic officers can do this, but this does not make them leaders. They are not necessarily those who speak publicly with eloquence and zeal—actors can do this, but this does not make them leaders.

Leaders are agents of change. Some leaders use the power given them to influence positive change in their spheres. Others use their fame to influence the opinion of others. Yet others maneuver their positions to force a result. There is even a type of leadership that employs wealth to acquire resources for some goal. As many styles as there are of leadership, all Christian disciples are called to leadership of one sort or another. The book of Nehemiah teaches us that we are to use authority, influence, fame, position, or wealth for the kingdom of God under the guidance of the Holy Spirit.

The temptation of leadership, though, is twofold. Some leaders fail through overstepping their jurisdiction, while others fail through not using the authority rightfully theirs. Let us study Nehemiah 5 to see how it illustrates these lessons of leadership.

inScribe

Write out Nehemiah 5 from the translation of your choice. If you're pressed for time, write out Nehemiah 5:6–8, 15, 19. You may also rewrite the passage in your own words, outline it, or mind map the chapter.

The Usage of Power

inGest

Go back to your scribed text and study the passage.

(Circle) repeated words/ phrases/ideas

Underline words/phrases that are important and have meaning to you

Draw **Arrows** to connect words/ phrases to other associated or related words/phrases

⟶

Memorize your favorite verse. Write it out multiple times to help memorization.

Where is accountability needed in your life? Public accountability? Spiritual accountability to God?

Read more at
www.inversebible.org/neh7-3

inTerpret

After looking at your scribed and annotated text, what special insights do your marks overall seem to point to?

←——————————————

What questions emerge after studying this passage? What parts are difficult?

What other principles and conclusions do you find?

Read more at
www.inversebible.org/neh7-4

The Usage of Power

inSpect

What relationship do the following verses have with the primary passage?

Rom. 12:14–21
1 Tim. 6:10
Acts 2:42–47; 20:32–38

⟶

What other verses/promises come to mind in connection with Nehemiah 5?

Review your memorized verse from Nehemiah 5.

Meditate on Nehemiah 5 again and look for Jesus in the chapter.

←————————————

How is Jesus like, as well as unlike, Nehemiah?

How do you see Jesus differently or see Him again?

Prayer: How do you respond to seeing Jesus in this way?

Read more at
www.inversebible.org/neh7-6

The Usage of Power

inSight

Review your memory verse.
How does it apply to your
life this week?

⟶

As you have studied this
week, what personal
applications have you been
convicted of in your life?

What are practical applications
you must make in your school,
family, workplace, and church?

Read more inSight from the
Spirit of Prophecy at
www.inversebible.org/neh7-7

inQuire

Share insights from this week's memory verse and Bible study as well as any discoveries, observations, and questions with your Sabbath School class (or Bible study group). Consider these discussion questions with the rest of the group.

←——————————————

Have you ever taken advantage of fellow Christians? In what ways?

How can we practice Christian principles like accountability in a secular world?

How can we practice accountability in the church?

Which is more difficult: using power at the right time or withholding power?

Is the larger culture more worried about personal rights or self-denial? How about you personally?

How should we avert internal crises in the local church today?

How can we emulate Christ's mind-set?

What examples have you seen of forbearance?

Through Hidden Opposition: Strength

Nehemiah 6:1–9

Week Eight

inTro

Read This Week's Passage:
Nehemiah 6:1–9

OVER THE MOUNTAIN

In chapter 4 Nehemiah encountered external opposition to his leadership over repairing the walls of Jerusalem. He then saw another obstacle when his own people halted the work due to social injustice in chapter 5. Like a bad rash, Sanballat, Tobiah, and their coconspirators are back in chapter 6, presenting additional complications! This time around, they do not attack Nehemiah directly but scheme a plot to get rid of him altogether.

If you see parallels, fear not; you are not seeing double. The pattern of the book of Nehemiah is a Hebrew chiasm (like an arch, or mountain). Chapter 4 is linked with chapter 6 about opposition. Later on, we will see chapter 3 linking with chapter 7 on organization; chapter 2 with chapter 8 on revival; and chapter 1 with chapter 9 on prayer. A chiasm leads up to the apex of the mountain, which tends to be the climax, or the most important focus of the narrative. In this case, the apex was chapter 5, which we studied last week. Ultimately, who does chapter 6 allude to? This week, we go down the mountain and retrace the themes that we saw on the way up.

inScribe

Write out Nehemiah 6:1–9 from the translation of your choice. If you're pressed for time, write out Nehemiah 6:1–5. You may also rewrite the passage in your own words, outline it, or mind map the chapter.

inGest

Go back to your scribed text and study the passage.

(Circle) repeated words/ phrases/ideas

Underline words/phrases that are important and have meaning to you

Draw **Arrows** to connect words/ phrases to other associated or related words/phrases

→

Memorize your favorite verse. Write it out multiple times to help memorization.

What should the Christian's response to personal attack be? To what extent are you responsible for how you are viewed by those around you?

Read more at
www.inversebible.org/neh8-3

inTerpret

After looking at your scribed and annotated text, what special insights do your marks overall seem to point to?

←————————————

What questions emerge after studying this passage? What parts are difficult?

What other principles and conclusions do you find?

Read more at
www.inversebible.org/neh8-4

Through Hidden Opposition: Strength

inSpect

What relationship do the following verses have with the primary passage?

Prov. 16:28; 17:9; 18:8
James 4:11
2 John 1:7–11

→

What other verses/promises come to mind in connection with Nehemiah 6:1–9?

Review your memorized verse from Nehemiah 6:1–9.

inVite

Meditate on Nehemiah 6:1–9 again and look for Jesus in the passage.

←——————————————

What parallels do you see between Jesus' response to temptation and Nehemiah's response?

How do you see Jesus differently or see Him again?

Prayer: How do you respond to seeing Jesus in this way?

Read more at
www.inversebible.org/neh8-6

inSight

Review your memory verse. How does it apply to your life this week?

⟶

As you have studied this week, what personal applications have you been convicted of in your life?

What are practical applications you must make in your school, family, workplace, and church?

Read more inSight from the Spirit of Prophecy at www.inversebible.org/neh8-7

inQuire

Share insights from this week's memory verse and Bible study as well as any discoveries, observations, and questions with your Sabbath School class (or Bible study group). Consider these discussion questions with the rest of the group.

←————————————————

What stands out to you in the chiasm of Nehemiah?

What are the Onos in your life?

Why is it so hard to say no?

What is the difference between obstinacy and discernment?

Though the story took place more than two millennia ago, how are things still exactly the same?

What are practical ways that we can seek the kingdom of God first?

Through Hidden Opposition: Discernment

Nehemiah 6:10–19

Week Nine

inTro

Read This Week's Passage:
Nehemiah 6:10–19

BLIND SIGHT

Modern medicine now has the ability to heal some forms of congenital blindness. The blind eye can be corrected through the use of latest restorative procedures. However, to the brain that has never seen the spectrum of the rainbow, the different intensities of light, and the various forms of shapes, nothing registers. Though the physical condition of the eye is functioning, the mind itself needs to be healed. Beyond the work of the physicians, the brain must be reprogrammed. So, when Jesus healed the boy who had been blind since birth (John 9), giving him the ability not only to see but to recognize everything, it was a tremendous miracle! Jesus not only healed his eyes but regenerated his mind, too.

Similarly, though our eyes might be functioning, we also need the miracle of sight. Not physical sight; our spiritual vision needs remedying so that we may discern different entities at work. Simple things like invitations, letters, and words may not be so simple. This week's lesson looks at two instances in Nehemiah 6 where the veil of blindness was lifted and discernment was granted.

inScribe

Write out Nehemiah 6:10–19 from the translation of your choice. If you're pressed for time, write out Nehemiah 6:12, 16. You may also rewrite the passage in your own words, outline it, or mind map the chapter.

inGest

Go back to your scribed text and study the passage.

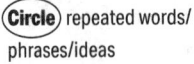 repeated words/phrases/ideas

Underline words/phrases that are important and have meaning to you

Draw **Arrows** to connect words/phrases to other associated or related words/phrases

Memorize your favorite verse. Write it out multiple times to help memorization.

How is your perception? Do you look beyond the surface in your relationships? Do you ask God to open your eyes to your own true condition?

Read more at
www.inversebible.org/neh9-3

inTerpret

After looking at your scribed and annotated text, what special insights do your marks overall seem to point to?

←—————————————→

What questions emerge after studying this passage? What parts are difficult?

What other principles and conclusions do you find?

Read more at
www.inversebible.org/neh9-4

inSpect

What relationship do the
following verses have with
the primary passage?

Deut. 13:1–5; 18:20
1 Cor. 2:14
Heb. 4:12; 5:14

→

What other verses/promises
come to mind in connection with
Nehemiah 6:10–19?

Review your memorized verse
from Nehemiah 6:10–19.

inVite

Meditate on Nehemiah 6:10–19 again and look for Jesus in the passage.

←────────────────

How did Jesus display the gift of discernment during His earthly ministry?

How do you see Jesus differently or see Him again?

Prayer: How do you respond to seeing Jesus in this way?

Read more at
www.inversebible.org/neh9-6

inSight

Review your memory verse. How does it apply to your life this week?

⟶

As you have studied this week, what personal applications have you been convicted of in your life?

What are practical applications you must make in your school, family, workplace, and church?

Read more inSight from the Spirit of Prophecy at www.inversebible.org/neh9-7

inQuire

Share insights from this week's memory verse and Bible study as well as any discoveries, observations, and questions with your Sabbath School class (or Bible study group). Consider these discussion questions with the rest of the group.

←—————————————

Are you a Tobiah who talks, or are you a Nehemiah who walks?

How should you meet personal attacks upon your work and/or character?

How can you influence others to work for Christ in a positive way?

How can prayer strengthen courage?

Who are other false prophets? What lessons do you learn from them?

When has fear overshadowed your faith?

When has mystical awe overshadowed your faith?

How do we keep faith always before us, especially in front of fear and awe?

What is your relationship with the Spirit of Prophecy?

Through Hidden Opposition: Discernment

Successors and Ancestors

Nehemiah 7

inTro

Read This Week's Passage:
Nehemiah 7

PIVOT TO PEOPLE

Up to this point in the book, Nehemiah had overcome many obstacles: external opposition from international coalition forces, internal social conflicts within the community, and the logistics of rebuilding the walls within two months! His answers to these issues were primarily prayer and dependence on God while maintaining his focus on the immediate work before him.

But aside from the immediate objective, Nehemiah's main purpose was still something higher—a purpose somewhat obscured from view until now. He was to rebuild not only Jerusalem but the people of Jerusalem. For what is a walled city without people to inhabit it?

Biblical leadership must always be concerned for people. While business, science, and politics focus on the objective leadership tasks at hand with values such as profit, progress, and power, biblical leadership always takes into account the people. We will discover that Nehemiah's leadership sought restoration of the community and its connection with God.

While the first six chapters of the book focused on the material restoration of the walls, chapters 8 through 13 now pivot to the spiritual restoration of the people.

inScribe

Write out Nehemiah 7:1–5 from the translation of your choice. You may also rewrite the passage in your own words, outline it, or mind map the chapter.

inGest

Go back to your scribed text and study the passage.

(Circle) repeated words/ phrases/ideas

Underline words/phrases that are important and have meaning to you

Draw **Arrows** to connect words/ phrases to other associated or related words/phrases

⟶

Memorize your favorite verse. Write it out multiple times to help memorization.

Where is accountability needed in your life? Public accountability? Spiritual accountability to God?

Read more at
www.inversebible.org/neh10-3

inTerpret

After looking at your scribed and annotated text, what special insights do your marks overall seem to point to?

←————————————————

What questions emerge after studying this passage? What parts are difficult?

What other principles and conclusions do you find?

Read more at
www.inversebible.org/neh10-4

inSpect

What relationship do the following verses have with the primary passage?

2 Tim. 2:2
Acts 6:1–7
1 Tim. 1:4

———————————→

What other verses/promises come to mind in connection with Nehemiah 7?

Review your memorized verse from Nehemiah 7.

inVite

Meditate on Nehemiah 7 again and look for Jesus in the passage.

←——————————————

Is Jesus exclusive? Is salvation exclusive?

How do you see Jesus differently or see Him again?

Prayer: How do you respond to seeing Jesus in this way?

Read more at
www.inversebible.org/neh10-6

Successors and Ancestors

inSight

Review your memory verse. How does it apply to your life this week?

⟶

As you have studied this week, what personal applications have you been convicted of in your life?

What are practical applications you must make in your school, family, workplace, and church?

Read more inSight from the Spirit of Prophecy at www.inversebible.org/neh10-7

inQuire

Share insights from this week's memory verse and Bible study as well as any discoveries, observations, and questions with your Sabbath School class (or Bible study group). Consider these discussion questions with the rest of the group.

←─────────────

Who will take up the work in your position after you?

Which is more difficult: competence or spirituality?

How do you respond to someone who simply won't stand down from their position to the detriment of the organization?

In what ways have we placed culture, race, or ethnicity above our Lord?

Are you meticulous and watchful with your spiritual life?

Are you watchful of the spiritual lives around you?

How can we better keep our finances and details as ordered as Nehemiah did?

What kinds of threats are around you constantly?

Recipe for Revival

Nehemiah 8

inTro

Read This Week's Passage:
Nehemiah 8

REVIVING REVIVALS

What is usually thought of when thinking about contemporary revivals? A renowned speaker, a large venue or facility with state-of-the-art sound systems and speakers, aggressive advertising on multiple platforms, wide-scale contiguous outreach activities, and magnificent music with recognized names are the usual components when putting a revival together. But what is it that makes a revival, a revival? Do all these peripheral elements define a revival? What does the Bible have to say about revivals?

Nehemiah 8 is the chapter where we find those answers. By God's grace, now that Nehemiah has taken care of the enemies, the wall, and the city, he moves on to the religious arena, seeking spiritual restoration. If you have been following along the chiasm of the book of Nehemiah, we started with prayer in chapter 1, revival in 2, organization in 3, and opposition in 4. We hit the apex in chapter 5 in the character and ministry of Jesus! We boomeranged back to opposition in 6, organization in 7, and now, again, revival in this chapter. (You can also guess what chapter 9 will be about!)

inScribe

Write out Nehemiah 8:1–8 from the translation of your choice. If you're pressed for time, write out Nehemiah 8:1–3, 8. You may also rewrite the passage in your own words, outline it, or mind map the chapter.

inGest

Go back to your scribed text and study the passage.

 repeated words/phrases/ideas

Underline words/phrases that are important and have meaning to you

Draw **Arrows** to connect words/phrases to other associated or related words/phrases

⟶

Memorize your favorite verse. Write it out multiple times to help memorization.

How can you experience personal revival? Is corporate revival possible? How can it be achieved?

Read more at
www.inversebible.org/neh11-3

inTerpret

After looking at your scribed and annotated text, what special insights do your marks overall seem to point to?

←——————————————→

What questions emerge after studying this passage? What parts are difficult?

What other principles and conclusions do you find?

Read more at
www.inversebible.org/neh11-4

inSpect

What relationship do the
following verses have with
the primary passage?

2 Chron. 7:14
Ezra 7:6–10
Acts 2

——————————→

What other verses/promises come
to mind in connection with

Review your memorized verse
from Nehemiah 8.

inVite

Meditate on Nehemiah 8 again
and look for Jesus in the passage.

←━━━━━━━━━━━━

Can there be true revival without
an encounter with Jesus?

How do you see Jesus differently
or see Him again?

Prayer: How do you respond to
seeing Jesus in this way?

Read more at www.inversebible.
org/neh11-6

Recipe for Revival

inSight

Review your memory verse. How does it apply to your life this week?

——————————→

As you have studied this week, what personal applications have you been convicted of in your life?

What are practical applications you must make in your school, family, workplace, and church?

Read more inSight from the Spirit of Prophecy at www.inversebible.org/neh11-7

inQuire

Share insights from this week's memory verse and Bible study as well as any discoveries, observations, and questions with your Sabbath School class (or Bible study group). Consider these discussion questions with the rest of the group.

←—————————

How are today's revivals the same as or different from what the Bible describes?

Are there counterfeit revivals? What do they look like?

Which ingredients are essential, and which are elective?

How does each phase of revival transition to the other?

Which phase is most lacking today? Why?

Why can daily devotional habits be so difficult?

How can the habit of daily devotions be cultivated?

How can biblical revivals themselves be revived?

Power of Remembrance
Nehemiah 9

inTro

Read This Week's Passage:
Nehemiah 9

BOOKENDS

If you have been following the chiastic structure of Nehemiah, we have come to the end. (You're thinking, "Wait, there are more chapters!" We'll come to those next week.) As the first chapter revealed the future course of Nehemiah's ministry through prayer, Nehemiah 9, the corresponding bookend chapter, reflects on the past course of God's people also through prayer. Whereas the first prayer was by Nehemiah alone on behalf of the larger community, this prayer is about the whole nation of which Nehemiah is merely a part.

Though the two prayers are different in trajectory and in breadth, they both retain the elements of adoration, confession, promises, and vision (see week 1). Fasting is mentioned in both chapters, alluding to the sincerity of seeking God's will. Both incorporate the Word of God: in chapter 1, Nehemiah claims promises he knows, while in chapter 9, they "read from the book of the Law of the LORD their God for one-fourth of the day" (verse 3, NKJV).

Both prayers reveal the importance of studying how God's hand has led in history. "We have nothing to fear for the future, except as we shall forget the way the Lord had led us, and His teaching in our past history" (Ellen G. White, *Selected Messages*, vol. 3, 162).

inScribe

Write out Nehemiah 9:26–38 from the translation of your choice. If you're pressed for time, write out Nehemiah 9:30–35. You may also rewrite the passage in your own words, outline it, or mind map the chapter.

inGest

Go back to your scribed text and study the passage.

 repeated words/phrases/ideas

Underline words/phrases that are important and have meaning to you

Draw **Arrows** to connect words/phrases to other associated or related words/phrases

Memorize your favorite verse. Write it out multiple times to help memorization.

Have you recently recounted God's work in your personal life? In your family? In your church?

Read more at
www.inversebible.org/neh12-3

inTerpret

After looking at your scribed and annotated text, what special insights do your marks overall seem to point to?

←————————————

What questions emerge after studying this passage? What parts are difficult?

What other principles and conclusions do you find?

Read more at
www.inversebible.org/neh12-4

inSpect

What relationship do the
following verses have with
the primary passage?

Exod. 2:23–25
Luke 17:32
Heb. 13:1–8

⟶

What other verses/promises come
to mind in connection with

Review your memorized verse
from Nehemiah 9.

Meditate on Nehemiah 9 again and look for Jesus in the chapter.

←——————————

How far back can you recount Christ working in your family history?

Take time now to reflect on the trajectory of God's hand in your personal life as well as in your spiritual community. What patterns emerge? What is the theology of salvation history in your life? How does this narrative fit into the larger narrative of the Adventist movement, the Christian church, and the great controversy?

Prayer: How do you respond to seeing Jesus work in your life?

inSight

Review your memory verse. How does it apply to your life this week?

————————————→

As you have studied this week, what personal applications have you been convicted of in your life?

What are practical applications you must make in your school, family, workplace, and church?

Read more inSight from the Spirit of Prophecy at at www.inversebible.org/neh12-7

inQuire

Share insights from this week's memory verse and Bible study as well as any discoveries, observations, and questions with your Sabbath School class (or Bible study group). Consider these discussion questions with the rest of the group.

←——————————————

Why is it important for leaders to reflect on the past?

How does a social media/tech-savvy culture erode the ability to reflect?

How can technology help us to reflect?

What powerful insights have emerged from studying how God has led in your life?

As much as forgetfulness has spiritual repercussions, in what ways can forgetting be beneficial?

What lessons can we learn from reflecting spiritually, personally, collectively, nationally, and as a church?

How can we stop forgetting God's goodness?

How does remembering God's character help us in future trials?

Legacy of Leadership

Nehemiah 13

inTro

Read This Week's Passage:
Nehemiah 10–13

SIGN HERE

Nehemiah 9 left off with the prayer of remembrance. Like the conclusion of the prayer of chapter 1, the latter prayer also concludes with a spirit of surrender. Verse 36 reads, "Here we are, servants today!" (NKJV). The corporate body enters into a covenant, or a contract, with God. Chapters 10–13 technically do not fit into the chiastic structure; they act more like appendices to chapter 9. Chapter 10 contains a list of names of those who essentially were signing off on the contract. These names included Nehemiah the governor, priests, Levites, and the leaders of the city.

From verse 28 to verse 39, chapter 10 then outlines four areas in which the people entered into an oath and the attending curses should these oaths be broken. The first area was the realm of marriage, where they promised not to marry the non-Judean people of the land (verse 30). The second was the keeping of the seventh-day Sabbath (verse 31). The third was the return of the tithe (verses 35–37). And the fourth was the care of the house of God (verses 38, 39).

Within the time frame of about twelve years, Nehemiah returned to the land of Judah and found every single covenant oath broken, in the opposite order of which they were made (like another chiasm!). What is a leader to do now?

inScribe

Write out Nehemiah 13:6–25 from the translation of your choice. If you're pressed for time, write out Nehemiah 13:14, 22b, 29, 31b. You may also rewrite the passage in your own words, outline it, or mind map the chapter.

inGest

Go back to your scribed text and study the passage.

(Circle) repeated words/phrases/ideas

Underline words/phrases that are important and have meaning to you

Draw **Arrows** to connect words/phrases to other associated or related words/phrases

⟶

Memorize your favorite verse. Write it out multiple times to help memorization.

Are there areas of compromise in your life? Do you see compromise creeping into your home life? Your church life?

Read more at
www.inversebible.org/neh13-3

inTerpret

After looking at your scribed and annotated text, what special insights do your marks overall seem to point to?

←——————————

What questions emerge after studying this passage? What parts are difficult?

What other principles and conclusions do you find?

Read more at
www.inversebible.org/neh13-4

inSpect

What relationship do the following verses have with the primary passage?

Gen. 1:1–2:25
Mal. 3:8–10
1 Pet. 2:21–25

→

What other verses/promises come to mind in connection with Nehemiah 13?

Review your memorized verse from Nehemiah 13.

inVite

Meditate on Nehemiah 13 again
and look for Jesus in the chapter.

←—————————————————

How does Christ's leadership
surpass that of Nehemiah?

How do you see Jesus differently
or see Him again?

Prayer: How do you respond to
seeing Jesus in this way?

Read more at
www.inversebible.org/neh13-6

Legacy of Leadership

inSight

Review your memory verse. How does it apply to your life this week?

⟶

As you have studied this week, what personal applications have you been convicted of in your life?

What are practical applications you must make in your school, family, workplace, and church?

Read more inSight from the Spirit of Prophecy at www.inversebible.org/neh13-7

inQuire

Share insights from this week's memory verse and Bible study as well as any discoveries, observations, and questions with your Sabbath School class (or Bible study group). Consider these discussion questions with the rest of the group.

←———————————————

How do we keep our eyes on Christ amidst the faults of human leadership?

Though Nehemiah may have been absolved from the curse of the covenant, what happened to the guilty people?

How does Christ come to take away the curse of the covenant?

Where is our house of God today?

Why is returning tithe difficult?

How does the Bible state we should keep the Sabbath properly?

Why is marriage under threat today?

How can we thank leaders biblically? Have you thanked or remembered your leaders recently?

How has Jesus practically been your personal leader?